This journal is dedicated to the loving memory of:

_____

Grief never ends...But it changes.
It's a passage, not a place to stay.
Grief is not a sign of weakness,
nor a lack of faith...It is the price of love.

Pain

I'm hurting alot today. I know I need to do something to get through this pain. I could go for a walk, have a massage, call up a friend, eat something delicious, listen to wonderful music, cook a meal for a friend, create something magical, take a child to a film, talk about you, watch a film we shared, call up your firends, look at old pictures, go to our favorite place, cry a little, cry a lot, pray, feel my courage, and I know you are near.

Here's what I am going to do

Secret thoughts

I know how you felt about me. Sometimes you didn't say it out loud, but I knew what you were thinking.

Mirrors

Here's what the inside of my head looks like.

My Birthday

Today is my birthday.

_____

_____

_____

_____

Today I feel

_____

_____

_____

_____

On my birthday you always used to

_____

_____

_____

_____

To celebrate my birthday, I will give myself a present from you

_____

_____

_____

_____

Holidays

Holidays are hard without you.

Today is

_____

_____

_____

_____

_____

_____

_____

_____

Here's what I am feeling without you today

_____

_____

_____

_____

_____

_____

_____

_____

Today is

_____
_____
_____
_____
_____
_____
_____

Here's what I am feeling without you today

_____
_____
_____
_____
_____
_____
_____
_____

The next time I am celebrating something big, please send me a sign from heaven that you are celebrating too. It will make the celebration that much sweeter when I record your sign here:

_____

_____

_____

_____

_____

_____

_____

_____

_____

Pain

I'm hurting alot today. I know I need to do something to get through this pain. I could go for a walk, have a massage, call up a friend, eat something delicious, listen to wonderful music, cook a meal for a friend, create something magical, take a child to a film, talk about you, watch a film we shared, call up your firends, look at old pictures, go to our favorite place, cry a little, cry a lot, pray, feel my courage, and I know you are near.

Here's what I am going to do

_____

_____

_____

_____

_____

_____

_____

_____

_____

_____

_____

_____

_____

_____

_____

_____

_____

_____

Secret thoughts

I know how you felt about me. Sometimes you didn't say it out loud, but I knew what you were thinking.

Mirrors

Here's what the inside of my head looks like.

My Birthday

Today is my birthday.

_____
_____
_____
_____

Today I feel

_____
_____
_____
_____

On my birthday you always used to

_____
_____
_____
_____

To celebrate my birthday, I will give myself a present from you

_____
_____
_____
_____

Holidays

Holidays are hard without you.

Today is

Here's what I am feeling without you today

Today is

Here's what I am feeling without you today

The next time I am celebrating something big, please send me a sign from heaven that you are celebrating too. It will make the celebration that much sweeter when I record your sign here:

Pain

I'm hurting alot today. I know I need to do something to get through this pain. I could go for a walk, have a massage, call up a friend, eat something delicious, listen to wonderful music, cook a meal for a friend, create something magical, take a child to a film, talk about you, watch a film we shared, call up your firends, look at old pictures, go to our favorite place, cry a little, cry a lot, pray, feel my courage, and I know you are near.

Here's what I am going to do

Secret thoughts

I know how you felt about me. Sometimes you didn't say it out loud, but I knew what you were thinking.

Mirrors

Here's what the inside of my head looks like.

_____

_____

_____

_____

_____

_____

_____

_____

_____

_____

_____

_____

_____

_____

_____

_____

_____

_____

_____

_____

_____

My Birthday

Today is my birthday.

Today I feel

On my birthday you always used to

To celebrate my birthday, I will give myself a present from you

----

Holidays

Holidays are hard without you.

Today is

Here's what I am feeling without you today

Today is

_____
_____
_____
_____
_____
_____
_____
_____

Here's what I am feeling without you today

_____
_____
_____
_____
_____
_____
_____
_____

The next time I am celebrating something big, please send me a sign from heaven that you are celebrating too. It will make the celebration that much sweeter when I record your sign here:

Pain

I'm hurting alot today. I know I need to do something to get through this pain. I could go for a walk, have a massage, call up a friend, eat something delicious, listen to wonderful music, cook a meal for a friend, create something magical, take a child to a film, talk about you, watch a film we shared, call up your firends, look at old pictures, go to our favorite place, cry a little, cry a lot, pray, feel my courage, and I know you are near.

Here's what I am going to do

_____

_____

_____

_____

_____

_____

_____

_____

_____

_____

_____

_____

_____

_____

_____

_____

_____

_____

Secret thoughts

I know how you felt about me. Sometimes you didn't say it out loud, but I knew what you were thinking.

Mirrors

Here's what the inside of my head looks like.

My Birthday

Today is my birthday.

_____

_____

_____

_____

Today I feel

_____

_____

_____

_____

On my birthday you always used to

_____

_____

_____

_____

To celebrate my birthday, I will give myself a present from you

_____

_____

_____

_____

Holidays

Holidays are hard without you.

Today is

Here's what I am feeling without you today

Today is

_____
_____
_____
_____
_____
_____
_____
_____

Here's what I am feeling without you today

_____
_____
_____
_____
_____
_____
_____
_____

The next time I am celebrating something big, please send me a sign from heaven that you are celebrating too. It will make the celebration that much sweeter when I record your sign here:

Pain

I'm hurting alot today. I know I need to do something to get through this pain. I could go for a walk, have a massage, call up a friend, eat something delicious, listen to wonderful music, cook a meal for a friend, create something magical, take a child to a film, talk about you, watch a film we shared, call up your firends, look at old pictures, go to our favorite place, cry a little, cry a lot, pray, feel my courage, and I know you are near.

Here's what I am going to do

Secret thoughts

I know how you felt about me. Sometimes you didn't say it out loud, but I knew what you were thinking.

Mirrors

Here's what the inside of my head looks like.

My Birthday

Today is my birthday.

_____

_____

_____

_____

Today I feel

_____

_____

_____

_____

On my birthday you always used to

_____

_____

_____

_____

To celebrate my birthday, I will give myself a present from you

_____

_____

_____

_____

Holidays

Holidays are hard without you.

Today is

Here's what I am feeling without you today

Today is

_____

_____

_____

_____

_____

_____

_____

_____

Here's what I am feeling without you today

_____

_____

_____

_____

_____

_____

_____

_____

_____

The next time I am celebrating something big, please send me a sign from heaven that you are celebrating too. It will make the celebration that much sweeter when I record your sign here:

_____

_____

_____

_____

_____

_____

_____

_____

Pain

I'm hurting alot today. I know I need to do something to get through this pain. I could go for a walk, have a massage, call up a friend, eat something delicious, listen to wonderful music, cook a meal for a friend, create something magical, take a child to a film, talk about you, watch a film we shared, call up your firends, look at old pictures, go to our favorite place, cry a little, cry a lot, pray, feel my courage, and I know you are near.

Here's what I am going to do

Secret thoughts

I know how you felt about me. Sometimes you didn't say it out loud, but I knew what you were thinking.

Mirrors

Here's what the inside of my head looks like.

My Birthday

Today is my birthday.

_____

_____

_____

_____

Today I feel

_____

_____

_____

_____

On my birthday you always used to

_____

_____

_____

_____

To celebrate my birthday, I will give myself a present from you

_____

_____

_____

_____

Holidays

Holidays are hard without you.

Today is

Here's what I am feeling without you today

Today is

Here's what I am feeling without you today

The next time I am celebrating something big, please send me a sign from heaven that you are celebrating too. It will make the celebration that much sweeter when I record your sign here:

_____

_____

_____

_____

_____

_____

_____

_____

_____

Pain

I'm hurting alot today. I know I need to do something to get through this pain. I could go for a walk, have a massage, call up a friend, eat something delicious, listen to wonderful music, cook a meal for a friend, create something magical, take a child to a film, talk about you, watch a film we shared, call up your firends, look at old pictures, go to our favorite place, cry a little, cry a lot, pray, feel my courage, and I know you are near.

Here's what I am going to do

Secret thoughts

I know how you felt about me. Sometimes you didn't say it out loud, but I knew what you were thinking.

_____
_____
_____
_____
_____
_____
_____
_____
_____
_____
_____
_____
_____
_____
_____
_____
_____
_____
_____
_____
_____

Mirrors

Here's what the inside of my head looks like.

_____

_____

_____

_____

_____

_____

_____

_____

_____

_____

_____

_____

_____

_____

_____

_____

_____

_____

_____

_____

_____

_____

My Birthday

Today is my birthday.

Today I feel

On my birthday you always used to

To celebrate my birthday, I will give myself a present from you

---

Holidays

Holidays are hard without you.

Today is

Here's what I am feeling without you today

Today is

_____
_____
_____
_____
_____
_____
_____
_____
_____

Here's what I am feeling without you today

_____
_____
_____
_____
_____
_____
_____
_____
_____

The next time I am celebrating something big, please send me a sign from heaven that you are celebrating too. It will make the celebration that much sweeter when I record your sign here:

_____

_____

_____

_____

_____

_____

_____

_____

Pain

I'm hurting alot today. I know I need to do something to get through this pain. I could go for a walk, have a massage, call up a friend, eat something delicious, listen to wonderful music, cook a meal for a friend, create something magical, take a child to a film, talk about you, watch a film we shared, call up your firends, look at old pictures, go to our favorite place, cry a little, cry a lot, pray, feel my courage, and I know you are near.

Here's what I am going to do

_____

_____

_____

_____

_____

_____

_____

_____

_____

_____

_____

_____

_____

_____

_____

_____

_____

_____

_____

Secret thoughts

I know how you felt about me. Sometimes you didn't say it out loud, but I knew what you were thinking.

Mirrors

Here's what the inside of my head looks like.

My Birthday

Today is my birthday.

_____

_____

_____

_____

Today I feel

_____

_____

_____

_____

On my birthday you always used to

_____

_____

_____

_____

To celebrate my birthday, I will give myself a present from you

_____

_____

_____

_____

Holidays

Holidays are hard without you.

Today is

Here's what I am feeling without you today

Today is

_____

_____

_____

_____

_____

_____

_____

_____

Here's what I am feeling without you today

_____

_____

_____

_____

_____

_____

_____

_____

The next time I am celebrating something big, please send me a sign from heaven that you are celebrating too. It will make the celebration that much sweeter when I record your sign here:

_____

_____

_____

_____

_____

_____

_____

_____

_____

Pain

I'm hurting alot today. I know I need to do something to get through this pain. I could go for a walk, have a massage, call up a friend, eat something delicious, listen to wonderful music, cook a meal for a friend, create something magical, take a child to a film, talk about you, watch a film we shared, call up your firends, look at old pictures, go to our favorite place, cry a little, cry a lot, pray, feel my courage, and I know you are near.

Here's what I am going to do

Secret thoughts

I know how you felt about me. Sometimes you didn't say it out loud, but I knew what you were thinking.

Mirrors

Here's what the inside of my head looks like.

My Birthday

Today is my birthday.

Today I feel

On my birthday you always used to

To celebrate my birthday, I will give myself a present from you

---

Holidays

Holidays are hard without you.

Today is

Here's what I am feeling without you today

Today is

_____
_____
_____
_____
_____
_____
_____
_____
_____

Here's what I am feeling without you today

_____
_____
_____
_____
_____
_____
_____
_____

Made in United States
Orlando, FL
16 January 2024

42563162R00072